EP Language Arts 7
Printables

This book belongs to:

_____

This book was made for your convenience. It is available for printing from the Easy Peasy All-in-One Homeschool website. It contains all of the printables from Easy Peasy's Language Arts 7 course. The instructions for each page are found in the online course.

Please note, in the various places where parts of speech are practiced, certain words can be categorized in more than one place (you can go for a swim [noun] or you can swim [verb]). If your child marks one of them differently than the answer key indicates, have a conversation with them to find out why.

Easy Peasy All-in-One Homeschool is a free online homeschool curriculum providing high quality education for children around the globe. It provides complete courses for preschool through high school graduation. For EP's curriculum visit allinonehomeschool.com.

EP Language Arts 7 Printables

ISBN: 9781091727083

First Edition: April 2019

Fix the errors you find in the following paragraphs. There are ten mistakes.

Marie Curie or Madame Curie as she is known to many was a scientist in the late 19th and early 20th centurys. Born in Poland, she moved to France to continue her scientific studies and ended up marrying a physics professor. The pear worked together for the advancement of science particularly physics.

Marie Curie shattered glass ceilings all over the place. She co-earned a Nobel Prize in 1903, making her the first woman ever to earn won. She went on to earn another one as well. After her husbands death, she took his place as professor of physics. She was the first women to hold the position.

Madame Curie is most known for her work with radium. Although exposure to the element eventually killed her her research leads to advancements in x-ray machines, which improve lives daily, almost a century after her death.

Fix the errors you find in the following paragraphs. There are ten mistakes.

At the end of World War II, Germany, as well as its former capital of berlin, was divided between the Allies and Russia. In the post-war period many people emigrated from the Russian side of East Germany too help rebuild the Allie's West Germany. The economy of East Germany suffered greatly from the lack of labor. In order to keep people from emigrating, as well as to protect their communist society from Western influence East Germany built a guarded brick wall in 1961 and topped it with barbed wire.

The wall was an immediate publicity catastrophe for East Germany and communism as a hole. The wall itself along with the very public punishments of those who tried to cross it showcased the tyranny of communism. Under U.S. pressure, the wall came down on November 9 1989 and within three years, all but three communist nations had collapsed.

Fix the errors you find in the following paragraphs. There are ten mistakes.

Jesse Owens was the grandson of a slave. Born in September of 1913 in Alabama Jesse was the youngest of ten children. Along with 1.5 million other african american's who were part of the "Great Migration," his family left the segregated south when he was nine years old and moved to Ohio in search of better opportunities. It was in Ohio that Jesse became a track and field star.

He was only in high school when he gained national attention for tying the world record in the 100 yard dash. At a college track meat, it took him less than an hours' time to break three world records and tie a forth. Then at the 1936 Olympics Jesse Owens achieved a feat no Olympian had ever achieved up to that point when he earned four gold medals. Jesses' performance undermined Adolf Hitler's ridiculous claims about racial superiority.

Fix the errors you find in the following paragraphs. There are ten mistakes.

Philip Sousa was born in Washington D.C. the third of ten children. When he was thirteen his father enlisted him in the Marine Corp too keep him from joining a circus band. He started as an apprentice with the Marine Band, and then he moved on two a theatrical orchestra where he learned to conduct. He then returned to the Marine Band as a conductor, going on to lead "The President's Band" under five presidents.

Sousa went on to be a composer of marches, earning him the nickname "the American March King". His most famous marches include the following the U.S. National March called "The Stars and Stripes Forever" and "Semper Fidelis" the official march of the U.S. Marine Corps. He eventually conducted his own band, named the Sousa Band, which featured a new instrument that most every marching band today uses — the aptly named sousaphone.

Fix the errors you find in the following paragraph. There are five mistakes.

Clive Staples Lewis is a well-known British author, most famous four his *Chronicles of Narnia* series of books. Through his Christian faith is evident throughout many of his writings C.S. Lewis actually left Christianity for atheism during his university years. However after years of intellectual wrestling Lewis returned to Christianity and became a great defender of the faith.

Identify the part of speech of the underlined word by writing it on the line.

That <u>jump</u> was the highest of the meet. _____

I'll let <u>myself</u> out. _____

I'd love to fly <u>among</u> the stars. _____

The <u>shining</u> sun blinded the driver. _____

That fruit salad <u>looks</u> delicious! _____

We're <u>very</u> late for the meeting! _____

Fix the errors you find in the following paragraphs. There are ten mistakes.

Leonardo da Vinci mite be one of the most underrated people in history. You probably know he was an artist particularly a painter and sculpter. But he excelled in many other areas as well. He was a scientist who specialized in anatomy geology and botany He was also a righter, a mathematician, a musician, an architect, an engineer, a cartographer, and an impressive inventor.

Da Vincis inventions were amazingly ahead of his thyme. He invented the predecessor to the modern-day tank centuries before cars were invented. He even invented a fully animated robot while living in the 1400s! But his most famous invention stemmed from his favorite area of study – aviation. His famous flying machine probably has his Renaissance neighbors thinking he was as batty as the winged night creatures he studied to design it!

Fix the errors you find in the following paragraph. There are ten mistakes.

Mary Elizabeth Bowser was a slave during the 1800's. As a young woman, she was freed by her owner and sent to a Quaker school where she learned to read and right. Once the civil war began her kind, former owner asked if she would help the union by spying on the Confederacy.

To do this, Mary had to pretend to be dim-witted and uneducated. She also had to go back to being treated like a slave, a life she had largely gotten a way from. She was hired by Jefferson Davis, the president of the Confederacy. Using her position within his home, she would eavesdrop on conversation's read private communication's and then relay the information to a fellow spy who posed as a baker making regular bread deliveries. More than 100 years later, Mary was inducted into the U.S. Army Military Intelligence Corps Hall of Fame for her efforts.

Fix the errors you find in the following paragraph. There are ten mistakes.

James Weldon Johnson was an african american born in the late 1800's to a society focused on segregating his people. However he knew very few boundaries in his life. He was able to get a college education, and he went on to be a grammar school principal. In 1897 he became the first African American to pass the bar exam in Florida.

A few years later James and his brother together rote the song "Lift Every Voice and Sing", which eventually became the official anthem of the National Association for the Advancement of Colored People (or the NAACP). President Roosevelt appointed Johnson to diplomatic positions in Nicaragua and Venezuela.

In a society that largely saw African Americans as subpar James Johnson defied the odds and lived an extrordinary life.

Fix the errors you find in the following paragraph. There are five mistakes.

The discovery of gold in California in 1848 changed the scope of many peoples lifes. Thousands migrated west, dreaming of the wealth that weighted beyond the horizon. Unfortunately, many dreamers lost everything. The cost of the supplies and the journey west squelched many dreams, before they really got started. Many even lost there lives chasing the riches.

Answer the following questions by selecting your choice from the answers given.

Which of the following sentences is an interrogative sentence?

a. I'm not sure what you're asking.   b. Please clarify your question.

c. Are you hungry?   d. I guess it's time for lunch.

What is the complete subject of this sentence? *Mary's teacher praised her efforts.*

a. Mary's teacher   b. Mary   c. praised   d. praised her efforts

What is the complete predicate of the same sentence?

a. Mary's teacher   b. Mary   c. praised   d. praised her efforts

Choose the simple subject and simple predicate of the same sentence.

a. Mary/efforts   b. teacher/praised   c. her/efforts

Use this organizing chart to map out your five paragraph essay.

Topic:		
Introductory paragraph:		
Paragraph 2	Paragraph 3	Paragraph 4
Main idea:	Main idea:	Main idea:
Supporting Details	Supporting Details	Supporting Details
Concluding paragraph:		

Lesson 40: Editing Checklist

Read through your essay and fix any mistakes. Here is an editing checklist. Aim for a check mark in each box.

Introduction
- [ ] My introduction begins with an attention grabber.
- [ ] My introduction has at least three sentences.
- [ ] My introduction ends with the main idea of my essay.

Body
- [ ] The body of my essay has at least three paragraphs.
- [ ] Each paragraph of the body starts with a topic sentence.
- [ ] Each paragraph of the body has at least three supporting sentences.
- [ ] Each paragraph of the body has a conclusion sentence.

Conclusion
- [ ] My conclusion has at least three sentences.
- [ ] My conclusion restates my main idea.
- [ ] My conclusion answers the question, "So what?"

Unity
- [ ] My essay flows well and makes sense.
- [ ] My essay uses connecting words to transition between paragraphs.
- [ ] My essay is interesting.

Subject Matter
- [ ] My essay has different sentences – short, long, compound, complex.
- [ ] My essay uses descriptive words.
- [ ] All parts of my essay support my main idea.

Grammar/Mechanics
- [ ] All words are spelled correctly.
- [ ] There are no grammatical mistakes.
- [ ] There are no punctuation errors.
- [ ] There are no fragments.
- [ ] There are no run-on sentences.

Fix the errors you find in the following paragraphs. There are ten mistakes.

Hedy Lamarr was an incredibly popular actress in the 1930's and 1940's. She had rolls opposite such popular stars as Clark Gable and Jimmy Stewart. Hedy was known as "The Most Beautiful Woman in Film" by her contemporaries.

However Hedy Lamarr was also incredibly intelligent. In 1942 along with her composer friend George Antheil Hedy patented what she called the "Secret Communication System". It was originally concocted to solve an issue in World War II where the Nazis were decoding messages and blocking signals from radio-controlled missiles. It involved changing radio frequencies so that enemies couldn't detect the messages in the first place. The later invention of the transistor catapulted Hedys' invention into practical space, and it is still used today in both military applications as well as sell phone technologys.

Write a summary of the story of Little Red Riding Hood.

_____

_____

_____

_____

_____

Fix the errors you find in the following paragraph. There are five mistakes.

Annie Oakley was forced to learn how to trap and shoot as early as age ate in order to support her family due to the death of her father. She became a fantastic shot while supporting her family and she went on to join Buffalo Bills Wild West show. Annie became a world-renowned rifle sharpshooter one of the best of all time. It is believed that she taught more than 15,000 woman to shoot a gun.

Fix the errors you find in the following paragraphs. There are ten mistakes.

In the 1950's, the space race was hot particularly between the united states and the Soviet Union. Each nation wanted to be the first one to do a certain thing in space. Some of the firsts were the first launch into space, first animal in space, first human in space, first human to orbit the earth, and others. When the Soviet Union started to get the lead in the race, the United States, in desperation, opened a project with one goal. They want to nuke the moon.

The precision was important. The whole point of nukeing the moon was making it visible to people. They planed to aim for the edge of the visible side of the moon. That way the cloud from the explosion would be illuminated by the sun and visible far and wide. Ultimately the project was abandoned do to concerns about contaminating space or the bomb detonating early and endangered the inhabitants of the earth.

Fix the errors you find in the following paragraphs. There are ten mistakes.

Famines can be caused by a lack of food or by a lack of access to food. There are many different causes of famines. Extreme whether plant diseases and animals can all cause a lack of food. Even goverments can cut off access to food, resulting in famine.

Throughout history, weather has impacted our food supply. During horrible freezes or severe droughts food prices in the United states and other civilized nations can skyrocket to compensate for the lack of crops. But in other areas of the world weather causes true famine. Sometimes plants get diseases that cause them to die, creating the same lack of crops that weather can create. Animals and bugs can eat and destroy crops as well.

The most surprising cause of famine is tyrannical leaders who keep food from there own people. Today many systems are in place to prevent governments from harming there own people in this way.

Fix the errors you find in the following paragraphs. There are ten mistakes.

Manfred Albrecht Freiherr von Richthofen was a fighter pilot for germany during World War 1. He became one of the most famous fighter pilots of awl time throughout the course of the war. Painting his aircraft red lead him to be called by the nicknames "Red Fighter Pilot", "Red Battle Flyer", and, most famously, "Red Baron".

The Red Baron was likely the deadliest fighter pilot in the entire war. He was officially credited with eighty air combat victories before his death. At one point during combat, a hit to the head caused him temporary blindness. He recovered well enough to successfully make a rough landing of his plane. Eventually however his reputation made him a very sought-after target. Everyone wanted credit for bringing down the Red Baron and its still unclear who ultimately put the permanent end to his combat career.

Fix the errors you find in the following paragraphs. There are ten mistakes.

The city of Jerusalem is a fascinating place. It's historical background makes it a huge tourist location, drawing people from all parts of the world. But its biggest lure comes from its religious roots. In Hebrew, Yerushalayim means "foundation of peace". This name might be considered ironic. Since the city of Jerusalem is considered by three of the worlds' largest religions to be there religious center, it has been the reason for many wars over the centuries.

Christianity Judaism and Islam all consider Jerusalem to be important to they're religion. Over the years, Jerusalem has seen the rise and fall of the kingdom of Israel, the death and resurrection of Jesus Christ, the Crusades, and many other so-called "holy wars." In fact Israelis and Palestinians continue to fight over the writes to occupy Jerusalem too this day.

Lesson 85: Rubric

Use this writing rubric to assess your essay.

	Advanced	Proficient	Basic	Below Basic
Ideas/ Content	☐ Literary elements such as character, plot, setting, conflict, etc. are well-developed around a central idea	☐ Literary elements such as character, plot, setting, conflict, etc. are somewhat developed around a central idea	☐ Literary elements such as character, plot, setting, conflict, etc. are unclear or leave too many questions	☐ Literary elements such as character, plot, setting, conflict, etc. are confusing or missing
Organi- zation	☐ Paper has an effective, great introduction ☐ Conclusion provides resolution ☐ Structure is creative and clear	☐ Paper has a good introduction ☐ Conclusion mostly provides resolution ☐ Structure is mostly creative and clear	☐ Introduction is present but unclear ☐ Conclusion doesn't resolve the problem or tell us what happens next ☐ Structure is loose	☐ Introduction is confusing or non-existent ☐ Conclusion is hasty or non-existent ☐ No obvious structure
Voice	☐ Writer's voice adds interest ☐ Point of view is skillfully expressed	☐ Writer's voice is fitting ☐ Point of view is evident	☐ Writer's voice is repetitive ☐ Point of view is confusing	☐ No sense of voice ☐ Point of view is missing
Word/ Language Choice	☐ Words are used appropriately ☐ Figurative language included	☐ Words are used well ☐ Descriptions are satisfactory	☐ Words and meanings are vague ☐ Descriptions lacking	☐ Limited vocabulary utilized ☐ Descriptive language absent
Sentence Fluency	☐ Sentence structure enhances story ☐ Transitions used between sentences and paragraphs	☐ Varied sentence structure evident ☐ Transitions present	☐ Sentence structure repetitive ☐ Limited transitional phrases	☐ Rambling or awkward sentences ☐ Transitions missing

Use this page to brainstorm for your essay. Jot down as many things as you can think of.

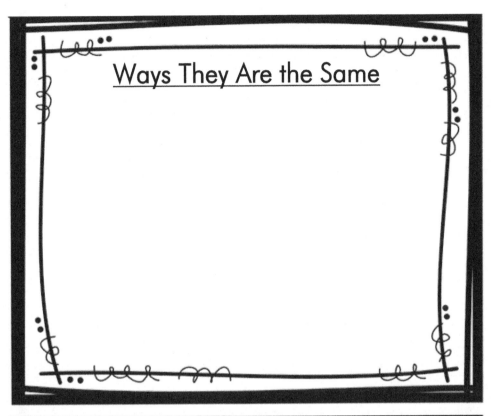

Ways They Are the Same

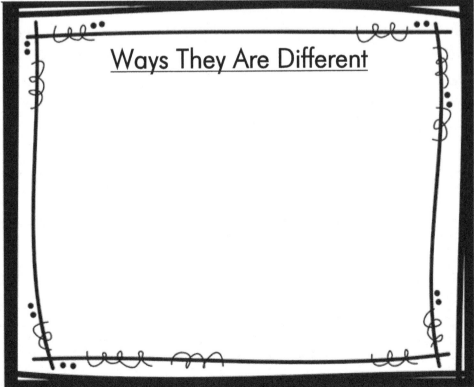

Ways They Are Different

Lesson 93: Proofreading

Rewrite the following paragraphs correctly. Be sure to proofread for errors in spelling, grammar, punctuation, capitalization, and usage.

Benjamin Franklin was a scientist inventor and writer. His most famous experiments dealed with electricity and he discovered many of it's governing laws. His work with electricity lead him to invent the lightening rod.

_____

_____

_____

_____

_____

Franklin is considered won of americas Founding Fathers. He lived in england for many years as a representative of the colonist's who had gone to america. Though he never saw miliarty action during the revolutionary war, he did sign both the declaration of independance and the united states constitution.

_____

_____

_____

_____

Lesson 94: Editing Checklist

Read through your essay and fix any mistakes. Here is your editing checklist again. Remember to aim for a check mark in each box.

Introduction
- ☐ My introduction begins with an attention grabber.
- ☐ My introduction has at least three sentences.
- ☐ My introduction ends with the main idea of my essay.

Body
- ☐ The body of my essay has at least three paragraphs.
- ☐ Each paragraph of the body starts with a topic sentence.
- ☐ Each paragraph of the body has at least three supporting sentences.
- ☐ Each paragraph of the body has a conclusion sentence.

Conclusion
- ☐ My conclusion has at least three sentences.
- ☐ My conclusion restates my main idea.
- ☐ My conclusion answers the question, "So what?"

Unity
- ☐ My essay flows well and makes sense.
- ☐ My essay uses transition words.
- ☐ My essay is interesting.

Subject Matter
- ☐ My essay has different sentences – short, long, compound, complex.
- ☐ My essay uses descriptive words.
- ☐ All parts of my essay support my main idea.

Grammar/Mechanics
- ☐ All words are spelled correctly.
- ☐ There are no grammatical mistakes.
- ☐ There are no punctuation errors.
- ☐ There are no fragments.
- ☐ There are no run-on sentences.

Lesson 95: Rubric

Use this writing rubric to assess your essay.

	Advanced	Proficient	Basic	Below Basic
Ideas/ Content	☐ Literary elements such as character, plot, setting, conflict, etc. are well-developed around a central idea	☐ Literary elements such as character, plot, setting, conflict, etc. are somewhat developed around a central idea	☐ Literary elements such as character, plot, setting, conflict, etc. are unclear or leave too many questions	☐ Literary elements such as character, plot, setting, conflict, etc. are confusing or missing
Organi-zation	☐ Paper has an effective, great introduction ☐ Conclusion provides resolution ☐ Structure is creative and clear	☐ Paper has a good introduction ☐ Conclusion mostly provides resolution ☐ Structure is mostly creative and clear	☐ Introduction is present but unclear ☐ Conclusion doesn't resolve the problem or tell us what happens next ☐ Structure is loose	☐ Introduction is confusing or non-existent ☐ Conclusion is hasty or non-existent ☐ No obvious structure
Voice	☐ Writer's voice adds interest ☐ Point of view is skillfully expressed	☐ Writer's voice is fitting ☐ Point of view is evident	☐ Writer's voice is repetitive ☐ Point of view is confusing	☐ No sense of voice ☐ Point of view is missing
Word/ Language Choice	☐ Words are used appropriately ☐ Figurative language included	☐ Words are used well ☐ Descriptions are satisfactory	☐ Words and meanings are vague ☐ Descriptions lacking	☐ Limited vocabulary utilized ☐ Descriptive language absent
Sentence Fluency	☐ Sentence structure enhances story ☐ Transitions used between sentences and paragraphs	☐ Varied sentence structure evident ☐ Transitions present	☐ Sentence structure repetitive ☐ Limited transitional phrases	☐ Rambling or awkward sentences ☐ Transitions missing

Lesson 100: Writing Organization

Choose six sentences from a recent writing assignment. Number the sentences, and fill in each column for each sentence. If you don't see a lot of variation in your writing, make some changes to make your writing more interesting.

Sentence Number	Number of Words	Sentence Type	Beginning Word	Connecting Word

This paragraph contains five misspelled words. Can you figure out what they are and spell them correctly on the lines?

When the original American colonists decided to revolt against British rule, there were many who were convinced the endeavor was destined for failure. Of course, without the benefit of hindsight, that feels like a fair assessment. After all, the colonists had an enormous undertaking to acomplish. They were attempting to addopt an entirely original form of government. They needed to addhere to a whole new adsortment of laws and legislations. While modern American leaders might agravate the world from time to time, the fledgling band of revolutionaries that started the United States achieved an incredible feat.

_____   _____

_____   _____

_____

Lesson 151: Spellcheck

This paragraph contains five misspelled words. Can you figure out what they are and spell them correctly on the lines?

Many scientists believe the world to be millions, if not billions, of years old. Various scientific publications repetedly state this as fact. However, there are a growing number of scientists who now believe the earth to be much younger than previously thought. Several dating methods have been proven to be inaccurate. Sometimes in science, the best we can do is speculait. Our speculations can coincied with available data, but no one can guarantie that their way is right. Altho some parts of our physical universe can be proven, many continue to be a mystery.

_____   _____

_____   _____

_____

A metaphor is where one thing is said to be another. Examples from *The King Will Make A Way*:

- She was always at work, an ant in an apron. (ch. 1)
- The sun was a brilliant gold medallion adorning the sky. (ch. 5)
- Outside the storm was a rampaging drunk, toppling everything within its reach… (ch. 5)
- (The character is looking at a tree): Her eyes opened and stared up at the wooden ladder. She wondered what she could see if she climbed limb by limb up the rungs to its top. (ch. 14)
- A line formed, an ever shifting centipede, a hundred legs taking little steps forward… (ch. 27)

Make some of your own metaphors. Finish these sentences. Example: Summer is a new toy fresh out of the box. Why is summer like a new toy fresh out of the box? It's something new and exciting. It's a time we break from routine and do something different. Don't just use a word or two, be creative!

Winter is _____

_____

Ice cream is _____

_____

My family is _____

_____

*Remember, a metaphor is saying one thing is something else. DO NOT use like or as. ("As sly as a fox" or "happy like a song bird" are examples of similes, not metaphors.)

(continued on next page)

Book genre simply means what type of book. Biography is a genre of nonfiction book that tells the story of a person's life. Other types of nonfiction book genres include reference, how-to, historic, scientific, sports, as well as many others.

Make a list of fiction genres you can think of: humor, western, _____

_____

_____

_____

Although not in its purest form, *The King Will Make a Way* is a type of allegory – one big metaphor. A metaphor is where one thing is said to be another. Some famous allegories are *Pilgrim's Progress* and *Animal Farm*. In *The King Will Make a Way* there is a King. He represents Jesus. The whole story you read in the book actually represents something else. As you read (if you're reading it), be mindful of the clues to show you what different things represent and what the story as a whole is about.

Choose a genre for your novel. Use the space below to write down any notes you'd like that pertain to your novel's genre.

_____

_____

_____

_____

_____

As a reminder, a **simple sentence** is simple – just one subject and predicate combination. *This is an example of a simple sentence.*

A **compound sentence** takes two simple sentences and compounds them, squashes them together using something like—"and", "or", "but"—in the middle to connect them. *This is an example of a compound sentence, and I have made it with two simple sentences joined together into one.*

A **complex sentence** takes a simple sentence and adds another subject and predicate in a way that they don't form another sentence on their own. *This is an example of a complex sentence because I have added a second subject and verb in a way that can't stand on its own.*

Identify these sentence types (from ch. 3 of *The King Will Make a Way*). The answers are simple, compound, or complex.

He crouched and examined mushrooms, pine cones, rocks and beetles.

_____

Gabe kept up the maneuvers until the guard was safely settled back in his guard box, comfortably seated on his stool.

_____

The toad hopped off just beyond him, and the natural impulse of a ten-year-old boy to try and catch it overpowered him.

_____

He looked up and his heart melted.

_____

Unthinking, he flung himself at the King's feet.

_____

Even though the hill was just a few stone throws away from the inn, he felt like a pioneer—adventurous and alone.

_____

Lesson 155: Descriptive Writing

Pick a place everyone in your family knows and describe it. Use all five senses. Don't use names or in any way tell them the answer in the description. See if they can figure out what you described.

_____

_____

_____

_____

_____

_____

Now write a description of a person everyone in your family knows. Again, don't give the answer, but describe the answer.

_____

_____

_____

_____

_____

_____

Lesson 156: Sentence Types

As a reminder, there are four types of sentences: declarative, interrogative, exclamatory, and imperative.

Declarative sentences make statements. *Today is my birthday.*

Interrogative sentences ask questions. *Is today your birthday?*

Exclamatory sentences exclaim. *Today is my birthday!*

Imperative sentences command. *Today's your birthday, so celebrate!*

Identify the sentence types of the sentences from chapter 5 of *The King Will Make a Way*.

He sat up straighter.   _____

When is it coming?   _____

Relax.   _____

What are you saying?   _____

Father was worried.   _____

Yes, sir!   _____

Get inside and stay there!   _____

This is going to be a bad storm!   _____

Tabitha shrieked.   _____

Remember the old village song?   _____

Lesson 157: Parallel Sentences

One way to show time passing quickly in your story is to use parallel sentences – sentences that have the same structure. Here's an example from chapter 6 of *The King Will Make a Way*: "The spring rain showered. The summer heat scorched. The fall apples ripened. The lake froze. The flowers bloomed. The corn was knee high. The harvest was gathered. Eggs hatched; bees buzzed; leaves tumbled."

Choose a time of year and write parallel sentences that tell your audience when you are talking about. It doesn't have to be a season. It could be Christmas time for example. Don't say it outright. Describe the time of year. Try to use all five senses!

_____

_____

_____

_____

_____

_____

_____

_____

Lesson 161: Irony • Oxymorons

Irony is when something is the opposite of what you would expect. A fire station catching on fire would be ironic. A murderer getting the death sentence as a punishment is ironic.

An **oxymoron** is when two contradictory terms are used together. Some examples are *jumbo shrimp, act naturally, only choice, alone together.*

Can you think of other examples of irony or oxymorons?

_____

_____

_____

_____

_____

_____

_____

_____

Lesson 163: Dialogue

Properly punctuate the dialogue at the top of the page. Then use the lines at the bottom of the page to write a dialogue of your own.

Come here he said

She got up and crossed the room What is it

A geode.

She asked again And that is what exactly

He brought out a hammer Watch and see.

_____

_____

_____

_____

_____

_____

_____

Add the missing punctuation to this sentence. Be sure to include any uncommon punctuation (semicolon, colon, dash).

I had too much on my mind so I got out of bed to make myself a list of what I needed to do call mom Jenny and the plumber bake the cookies take pictures of the kids and update the blog just so I could get some sleep

Write a sentence or a paragraph that uses a semicolon, a colon, and a dash.

_____

_____

_____

_____

_____

_____

Lesson 165: Metaphor

Find examples of metaphor in a book you are currently reading and write them on the lines. Come up with your own examples of metaphors if you'd like. Can you incorporate some metaphor into your novel?

Here's an example from *The King Will Make a Way*:

> "He knew of their meetings and their disloyalty, but they were a bunch of weaklings: women, children and old men, only a few straggly others joined them. There were the rooks, his guards; the queen, his devoted servants whom he could bid come to his side at a moment's notice; and he, of course, was the king. That left the knights, those horses that fancied themselves special—the only pieces on a chess board allowed to jump over another."

_____

_____

_____

_____

_____

_____

_____

_____

Anthropomorphism is a literary device where something non-human becomes humanlike in form and/or behavior. Read this sentence from chapter 15 of *The King Will Make a Way*:

> *Despair circled Gabe like a vulture, taunting, laughing. "He's dead. He's dead. They're all dead. Lifeless bodies left for the birds. You might as well join them. Vulpine will be after you next."*

What nonliving thing is taking on human attributes? _____

What human qualities did it have? _____

_____

Now you try it. Look at the pen or pencil in your hand. Make it come alive. What is it thinking as you are holding it, writing with it? What would it say when you are chewing on it, tapping it? Give it a personality and write a little story with the pen or pencil as the main character. Give his point of view on the world.

_____

_____

_____

_____

_____

_____

_____

Lesson 167: Lie vs. Lay

In the present tense, lie is what you do to yourself, and lay is what you do to something else. Fill in these blanks with lie or lay:

I _____ on my bed to rest.

A chicken _____s an egg.

In the past tense, lie becomes lay, and lay becomes laid. Fill in these blanks with lie, lay, or laid:

I want to _____ down for a nap.

Last week I _____ out the pattern for the dress.

I need to _____ out the schedule for everyone to see.

He _____ there for hours yesterday.

See if you can figure out the correct word for each blank.

My cat is _____ in the light.
  ○ laying   ○ lying

She often _____ there.
  ○ lies   ○ lays

I _____ my toothbrush on the sink.
  ○ lay   ○ laid

The US _____ to the north of Mexico.
  ○ lies   ○ lays

Lesson 171: Personification

Personification is when something inanimate is described as if it were animate. Here are some weather examples:

A soft rain tiptoed across the lawn.
The snow threw a white blanket over the lawn.
The sun smiled down on the lawn.

Choose a type of weather (sunny, windy, rainy, cloudy...) and describe what is happening using personification. Use the examples above to help you. Then do it again with another type of weather.

_____

_____

_____

_____

_____

_____

_____

_____

_____

_____

Alliteration is the repeating of the initial consonant sound in a series of words. Familiar examples might include Mickey Mouse, Donald Duck, or Peter Piper picked a peck of pickled peppers.

Write ten alliterations. Write at least two with 3 words and two with 4 words. See how many words you can string together in your longest one.

1. _____

2. _____

3. _____

4. _____

5. _____

6. _____

7. _____

8. _____

9. _____

10. _____

Lesson 178: Onomatopoeia

Onomatopoeia is when the name of the sound is associated with the sound. Words that make the sound they describe would be another way to say it. Here are some examples: bam, clatter, clap, mumble, pop, swoosh, rattle, thud, shuffle, whisper, buzz.

Write a short story about a morning in your home, from the time you get up until breakfast. Use as many sound words as you can in your story.

_____

_____

_____

_____

_____

_____

_____

_____

_____

_____

_____

Made in the USA
Coppell, TX
03 August 2020